# The Nurse First Handbook: Practical Solutions to Address Healthcare Burnout and Work-related Stress

Author: Dr. Shara Rhodes, DNP, RN, NEA-BC, MEDSURG-BC, NPDA-BC ®

# A much-needed and refreshing perspective on the urgency of burnout as a threat to the nursing industry

- *David L. Carter -*

Core principles:

- Recognition of burnout symptoms
- Reacting appropriately and healing measures
- Collaborative prevention techniques
- Reducing the need for resilience

# Table of Contents

For my children: Ravyn, Sydney and Ethan

*You inspire me to be the best human version of myself possible to make the world better for you. I love the brilliant person inside each of you.*

# Foreword: Nurse Wellbeing, A Chronic Problem

The first time I can remember experiencing burnout as a nurse was only slightly different than any other night. On this particular evening I was just returning from vacation time off with my family. My husband and I had taken the children and my mother on a trip to the beach. I had loved every minute of our trip and the kids were finally old enough to appreciate all of the fun of a family vacation, so we'd made some adorable memories.

As I drove onto campus for my shift and thinking about those sweet memories we had made, I was startled to realize there were tears streaming down my face. It struck me that these were not tears of joy. In fact, soon I was sobbing uncontrollably in my car. I pulled over into one of the parking lots and laid my head against the steering wheel. As I sat there,

I thought about the night ahead of me. I imagined there would be a waiting room full of unhappy patients, who had probably been waiting since daylight, all wondering when they would be called back for treatment. I was pretty sure someone had called out "sick" for the night, certain of at least one particular person who was known for not being at work as scheduled. I thought about which providers I would be managing on that shift. While I had come to really love working with each of them, navigating their different personalities and expectations had become a game that most of us were used to on our nursing team. Quite frankly, sometimes managing the providers' needs could be downright exhausting.

In that moment, in that parking lot, on that night, there was nothing more that I wanted to do than turn my car around, drive straight home, and never work another shift in the service of others. I felt detached, emotionally exhausted, and empty inside. I had no idea how I was going to go on as a nurse, in the profession that so many of my friends and family members had chosen. I was disappointed in myself. I had invested so much of my time and energy, many of my children's toddler years, and so much passion into the journey of becoming a nurse. Yet still, the joy I felt on the night of my pinning ceremony less than ten years prior, seemed like a distant memory that now belonged to someone else. That was it. I was burned out.

# How the Evidence Stacks Up

Many years late, I have come to realize my story is not uncommon compared to others I have heard in the years since that night. The threat of healthcare burnout impacts a bewildering percentage of nurses of varying experience levels, practice settings and educational backgrounds. A literature review of the scope of the problem provided thousands of sources documenting the impacts and significance of the issue. General statistics reflect a majority of nurses have self-reported feelings or symptoms of burnout which affect professionals across all healthcare genres in the industry (Chen, Strasser, Dent, Blanchard, Portela-Martinez, et al, 2024). A date-restrictive search of evidence pertaining to the issue of burnout resulted in more than 7,000 sources from 2024 alone. To focus the search, use of the more specific terms of "nursing burnout in the acute care setting" produced approximately 2,600 results published in 2024. Extensive evidence exists regarding the depth and range of burnout in the contemporary workforce. The search was further restricted by selecting only full-text peer-reviewed articles or scholarly textbooks used to define the characteristics of nurse burnout, and identify evidence-based practices for prevention, reduction and treatment. Finally, to further clarify actionable objectives, the scope of the search was limited to publications with specific guidance within three specific areas. The new parameters were used to focus the discussion on crafting a solid definition of the problem, prescribing educative measures on the characteristics of burnout, and implementing supportive measures to deconstruct factors which continually lead to reported burnout.

Additional exploration of the research was helpful in clarifying the scope of the issue. Potential impacts of healthcare burnout or compassion fatigue can include threats to both the affected employee as well as those with whom they interact. Similar to ongoing research about the nursing shortage, which has now compounded to approximately half a million nurses and care partners, burnout in healthcare workers has a long-documented history. Christensen, A.J., Virnig, J.P., Case, N.L., Hayes, S.S., Heyne et al reported increased potential for care delivery errors, escalating loss of productivity, and increased costs of care overall due to systemic burnout

(2024). Additionally, a continuous cycle has been linked to nursing leadership in some models, as both directly lending to and concurrently experiencing nursing burnout (Figure 1). Some describe the contribution made by poor leadership to employees becoming burned out. There is also evidence which signifies the staggering effects, such as physical and emotional exhaustion, that being a leader has on those who hold management positions. Both of these concepts are important to the science of burnout prevention.

There are many terms used to describe and define healthcare burnout. Literature suggests as a compilation of symptoms, burnout is best described as a multidimensional and complex condition of reduced connection to joy in the workplace (Schmidt SL, da Silva Cunha B, Tolentino JC, Schmidt MJ, Schmidt GJ et al, 2024). Cognitive, emotional and physical side effects also comprise well-documented literature regarding the configuration of symptoms used to describe the disconnection from caregiver compassion which typically accompanies burnout.

Figure 1.

# Burnout, Compassion Fatigue, Emotional Exhaustion and Other Names

What is the point of genesis of nursing burnout science? While the concept is well-researched, the answer to this question is widely debated. The importance of calling out compassion fatigue and other symptoms amounting to burnout has not been understated. Some elements of healthcare-related stress can be traced back to academia.

Annually, thousands of nursing students enroll in and graduate from institutions charged with the task of equipping them with foundational didactic knowledge to practice as a clinician. While the range of education delivery methods and institutional mission statements vary, the primary focus remains on delivering clinically-knowledgeable workers to provide care for those in need. More advanced institutions may even equip nurses with the competence to perform relatively independent at the time of graduation. Nursing school has often been heralded for its rigorous training, difficult tests and numerous levels of task completion to achieve success. The inclusion of resiliency strategies to recognize, prevent and overcome burnout has not been widely reported as a requirement for completion of study. In fact, many nursing students may arrive at the doors of their initial workplace already in a state of burnout from the difficulty of completing nursing school and passing their licensure exams.

While nursing is a career field with a solid foundation in the global workforce, the discipline continues to be plagued by factors contributing to an unyielding worker shortage. Further, burnout is still a primary causative factor to nurses leaving the field. In the healthcare industry alone, it affects millions of nurses practicing across multiple fields within and external to patient-facing organizations. Conservative estimates negate substantive differences in pre- and post-pandemic levels of healthcare burnout although there appears to be congruence in the characteristics of burnout, and agreement in its detriment to society. A 2023 study published by Wang, Zhang, Zhang et al included 1,584 subjects and used a "...stratified cluster sampling method..." to identify worker-reported symptoms of burnout (2024). The authors were able to confirm additional impacts such as components of chronic stress and post-trauma syndromes experienced by nurses currently within the workforce.

There are multiple phrases and terms used to describe the phenomenon of healthcare burnout. Worker exhaustion syndrome, compassion fatigue, nursing fatigue, and avoidable suffering are parallel terms which can be used to describe an unhealthy relationship to one's work. Contributing factors can include workplace violence, moral distress, inadequate care delivery environments, and ethical concerns for various conditions encountered throughout the course of a typical shift.

The amount of literature defining and characterizing burnout in nursing is staggering. Despite this, organizations still struggle to deconstruct and combat the forces surrounding this syndrome of exhaustion. Though the symptoms present as uniquely as each individual experiencing them, the defining characteristics remain the same and contribute to a similar constellation of responses.

In general terms, healthcare workers experiencing professional burnout have reported an array of symptoms such as:

- Physical and emotional exhaustion

- Problems with physical health

- Feelings of isolation and depersonalization

- Reduced performance

- Decreased satisfaction

- Clinically-relevant symptoms of
  depression or anxiety

The organizational responsibility to manage burnout of healthcare workers is an often overlooked and under-fulfilled component of healthcare strategy. Reactive methods such as workplace-sponsored mental health counseling and listening sessions have not fully proven to be directly beneficial to the many nurses who depart their nursing careers annually due to burnout. As natural nurturers, healthcare workers often choose to self-manage their symptoms of compassion fatigue, rather than taking advantage of passive solutions. Some examples of passive solutions can include those which are considered "self-service" products, typically not embedded in the workplace culture, and under-endorsed by leaders. These solutions are often reportedly underutilized because they are difficult to locate and navigate. The likelihood of nurses making use of these types of initiatives is even lower when there are complexities which make help seem elusive and unattainable (Image 1).     Symptom recognition can help healthcare workers and leaders to identify needs early, when prevention or intervention strategies are more likely to be successful. All stakeholders should be aware of the defining characteristics and causative factors of compassion fatigue, a phrase akin to workforce burnout. In some organization, leaders are incentivized to emphasize the use of wellbeing resources by their staff, using rewards and recognitions by senior leaders. These incentives are often highlighted with internal wellness metrics used to illustrate the health of the organization and effectiveness of assistance programs. Efforts to understand and dismantle the contributors to healthcare fatigue should be ongoing and assertively present within organizational strategy. Use of concerted efforts and investments in resources such

Image 1.

as software-engineered intelligence may prove successful in ending the struggle and improving industry retention. Reducing the risk of workers ever becoming burned out can be one of the most important investments an organization can make in sustaining its workforce.

# Systemic Education to Define Nursing and Healthcare Worker Burnout, and Prepare Stakeholders to Recognize the Symptoms and Risk Factors

Healthcare worker burnout can be unrecognizable and easily mistaken for something else. Nurses may exhibit changes in behavior such as increased tearfulness, use of alcohol, dry humor or increased attendance issues. Although I was experiencing spectacular symptoms of burnout on that pivotal night as I returned from vacation time off, it would take me years to explore what happened to me and come to actually give it a name. I continued my drive to work, got to my building, and heaved myself into the work. That night I began applying for other jobs throughout my organization's network. By the end of the month I had applied to more than thirty jobs, was invited to interview for nearly two dozen positions, and had received multiple competing offers. I decided on a position that was new to me clinically but required little effort matching my qualifications and background. It was a role that I have now come to refer to as a "brief sabbatical" in my nursing career. It allowed me to spend extra time with my family, rediscover a love for nursing, and establish a new connection in an environment which personally brought me joy as a clinician.

After less than a year into my "brief sabbatical" I felt I was ready to get back to the grind of nursing, and switched gears again. I quickly assumed a more challenging role without ever exploring what had truly brought me to need to break away from my previous life and work. I simply continued my journey, settled into my new career, and heaved myself into the work yet again. Because of this failure to fully explore and heal in this period in my life, there would be at least two additional times in my career when I would question if nursing was still my calling.

Chronic occupational distress is a byproduct of continuous exposure to flaws and breakdowns in care environments. Repeated or intense exposure without alleviating factors is often linked to diminished capacity for managing stress. This chronic, poorly-managed stress can be a primary risk factor for developing symptoms of burnout in those working in healthcare occupations. Nurses and nursing professionals are especially prone to compassion fatigue and moral distress

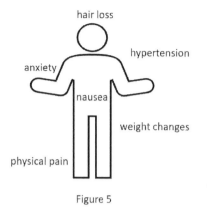

hair loss

hypertension

anxiety

nausea

weight changes

physical pain

Figure 5

because of their repeated proximity to chronic occupational stress. Burnout is a multidimensional syndrome characterized by changes in energy, performance, and emotional response to workplace triggers. A close assessment of the clinical picture of a nurse who is experiencing the physical and mental exhaustion of being burned out is important in the healing journey (Figure 5). Immersive learning strategies such as role play and visual reflective strategies can help clinicians connect their own symptoms with the educative experience. Understanding the symptomatology of healthcare worker distress is essential to overcoming its effects. This understanding can be accomplished with systemic educational efforts to ensure stakeholders are aware of the definition of burnout, and can properly distinguish the markers of a worker who is burned out.

Education about healthcare worker fatigue can be a powerful approach to decreasing knowledge deficits in the workplace setting. The use of appropriate delivery methods, development of relevant content, and application of effective engagement strategies can enhance the success of education delivery. Knowledge deficits in the definition of healthcare burnout have been sharply addressed in recent years. For clarity, the definition of burnout, while well-documented, is not necessarily universal language for all stakeholders. The range of sources available to stakeholders in defining burnout is quite expansive. However, the definition of burnout within an organization should be connected to the mission statement and encompassing all employees who are primarily at risk for its effects.

Primary stakeholders, while inclusive of the employee or group of employees experiencing burnout and their leaders, can also extend beyond the initial layer of impact. Preceptors, educators, ancillary or supplementary departments, students, instructors, and many others can be seen as stakeholders in programs used to address burnout. Each of these individuals and teams should be educated about the symptoms and effects of burnout. It is imperative that all stakeholders are provided with protective resources to aid in preventing or resolving their own burnout. Education should include instruction, demonstration, and een return demonstration on how to access and use protective resources. Learners should also be evaluated collectively and individually for evidence of workplace factors which could contribute to threats to their wellbeing. This information can also be analyzed and used by executive leaders to form and sustain organizational strategic plans focusing on employee wellness.

As stakeholders, Preceptors are often considered to be the gatekeepers of the unit culture. Preceptor education can include a module on classic signs and symptoms of healthcare worker fatigue. These work-based trainers can be taught to recognize and report symptoms observed in new hires, to their leaders or education partners. A clear and easy-to-follow escalation pathway could consist of a daily review of the new hire's coping as they adapt to the work environment, along with established protocols for reporting their responses. Preceptors can also be used to train their peers on the availability of resources to support healthy workplace environment and individual wellbeing. Information sheets should be easy to read and can even include more advanced technologies such as QR codes which can be scanned for at-the-fingertips access to help when needed. In lieu of, or in addition to Preceptors, a unit-based education champion could be helpful in disseminating information about what burnout is, how to recognize it, who to contact when witnessed or experienced, and when to elevate concerns.

Partners in education are an extension of the clinical practice environment. Students and instructors should receive information about how the facility is combatting burnout by equipping stakeholders with the knowledge and tools to overcome this avoidable suffering. Sharing information such as this can not only impact organizational response to stressors, but can also have effects into the larger community who interacts with the organization. Educating students on the triggers, symptoms, and effects of burnout can aid in their recognition of gaps in wellbeing within themselves, their fellow students, and caregivers with whom they interact at the facility. It can also help to expand on their academic career in terms of building their knowledge and comfort level in preventing burnout in the future. Organizational leaders and their academic partners can work together on the content and delivery of educational information regarding burnout. Initial and ongoing assessment of knowledge, use of protective measures and communication pathways should be monitored collaboratively to determine gaps in both the professional and academic environments.

Education of collaborative partners outside of nursing is necessary for team cohesion at the organizational level. While working as a frontline caregiver I once witnessed an altercation between a peer and a technician working in telemetry monitoring. Later, I myself encountered the same technician as one of my patients exhibited a rhythm change. Upon initially answering my phone, the technician was quite hostile in alerting me that my patient's monitor was reading atrial fibrillation with a rapid ventricular rate. I responded by thanking her for the notification, and assured her that I would investigate right away. After assessing and treating my patient, I decided to call the technician back. When she answered, she was still somewhat hostile. I took a moment to introduce myself and let her know I was calling to close the loop regarding a patient she and I had collaborated on earlier, using this exact terminology. I thanked her for alerting me again and asked her to verify she could still see my patient's rhythm. Together we confirmed the patient's rhythm and by the end of a phone call lasting less than two minutes, she was upbeat and thanking me for calling her back to verify. "I am so glad you aren't burned out like your coworkers down there!" she said as we ended the call.

This brief encounter, although it started off rocky, might have been a healing interaction for this colleague. More importantly, it forced me to take a look at those I worked with on the unit, to consider if in fact they were experiencing any symptoms of burnout which were being weaponized against ancillary teams. Ensuring our colleagues outside of nursing are educated on the symptoms of burnout can actually have positive affects in how they interact with nurses and nursing teams. However, failing to equip these individuals and teams with the knowledge of how to verbalize their concerns for staff burnout could prove to be counter-effective. While this technician could recognize what likely was burnout in my nursing colleagues, because she did not know the appropriate person to convey those concerns to, she continued to expose herself to their disengaged and unhappy responses when it was necessary to interact with them.

Organizations must not limit education about the harmful effects of burnout to nurses and nursing teams. Sharing this knowledge with those away from the bedside can be an added layer of support to frontline caregivers. Ensuring targeted and role-specific education is provided can enhance the team culture. Widespread training on protective resources and response mechanisms can create a safe workplace environment and decrease the amount of time of avoidable suffering an individual or team might experience in burnout. Education and training can be provided during new hire orientation or onboarding, at regular intervals throughout the performance year, and as needed to address symptomatology. Education can be information-based, action-based, inclusive of dialogue or group discussions, and customized for specific populations.

# Routinization of a Sentinel Response to Care and Treatment of Healthcare Workers Experiencing Avoidable Suffering

Several years, and multiple career advancements along the way, I had the opportunity to reflect on my journey through nursing. At the time I was working as a freelance consultant in a small nonprofit organization and preparing for a presentation on workforce development. Part of my research involved the anthropological study of how human factors and organizational culture influence shifts in the workforce. The landmark "Institute of Medicine" report of 2010 brought a new face to healthcare by asserting "...that achieving a successful health care system in the future rests on the future of nursing" (Fineberg, n.d., as cited in IOM, 2011). The same report was used to place a call to action on healthcare to heed a terrible and deep shortage within the nursing workforce, and was also the basis for much of my work in workforce development.

As a researcher, my work focused at the time on uncovering the factors responsible for increasing attrition and the greater nursing shortage, both of which had continued to grow despite what we thought at the time were important countermeasures. In my studies I encountered concepts such as bullying and toxic culture, which were not foreign terms to me. Additionally, in studying the anthropology of these individual concepts, it became necessary to create a framework for a more urgent relationship with why people were leaving roles in nursing that they had previously loved. In gaining a more educated appreciation for the symptoms, it was clear the problem was there under the surface all along. Burnout had become a raging problem that many were unaware of and most of us were likely afraid to admit we knew little about.

I pressed in to the topic, and it dawned on me that many nurses I knew personally had exhibited classic symptoms of burnout, which we had sometimes even joked about together. I thought about the nurse whose fatigue with compassion was covered up in dry wit as she ruminated about the old days with stoic cynicism. Then there was the nurse who found herself near tears almost daily as she argued with those around her, about anything - big or small, likely attributed to (and often voiced in) her dissatisfaction with the workplace. I recalled the person I could count on with nearly pinpoint precision to call out on a weekend shift with barely veiled reasons, until he was chronically out of paid days off, and eventually terminated. I even thought about the coworker who had fallen and injured herself but kept working for nearly a year with a literal broken back, because her body was so chronically in pain from being a healthcare worker that she didn't recognize the seriousness of the new injury. With a sort of sadness and quiet alarm, I began to see glimpses of each of these nurses I knew and loved...in me. Not only had our organization failed to see that we were burned out and suffering, we had even failed to recognize it in each other.

The onset of worker burnout is not a terminal condition. While preventive tactics are an incredibly important contributor to diminishing the crippling effects of this syndrome, it is not a singular measure. As a multidimensional construct, healthcare burnout can manifest in varying degrees or stages, and can elicit diverse exhibitions based on the individual's unique inherent coping mechanisms. A nurse who is emotionally disconnected to the work may feel no guilt associated with chronically calling out and leaving her team short-staffed. Another who is emotionally exhausted by the work may seek shelter in stoic and cynical antics used to depict times when he felt energized as a nurse. Often the reaction to burnout recognized in another individual is similar to the popular adage "Don't ask, don't tell". Even when nurses are able to identify with and name burnout as their captor, sometimes it can be difficult to respond appropriately to the effects.

An appropriate response to the recognition of the symptoms and effects of this condition is necessary for adequate recovery (Image 2). Leaders should simplify methods to address nursing fatigue in order to amplify tactics to address burnout in caregivers.

Complex measures which are hard to access and navigate can sometimes be more damaging than lack of resources altogether. Despite the widespread impacts of healthcare worker burnout there is an urgent need to institute prevention methods and treat those currently experiencing burnout. When not addressed properly, the lived trauma can lead to errors in care delivery, turnover in roles and industry, and the potential for self-harm of nurses.

A sentinel response is one in which there are concentrated and coordinated efforts to observe, react, evaluate and study an important issue. This response is a confluence of intentional acts by interested parties who have recognized a problem, understand its detriment to the organization, and are deeply committed to preventing its reoccurrence. The timing, energy, and extent to which symptoms of burnout are addressed can lead to both short-term and long-term impacts for an individual and the organization with which they are associated.

In my studies I happened to interact with an organization who used a system called a "Code Teal" for healthcare worker resilience. This code, when activated, triggered a multidisciplinary chain of events including a team of colleagues coming together with refreshments, positive energy, physical touch, and uplifting affirmations. The code can be triggered by someone for themselves, by concerned coworkers who are worried about their colleague, or by others within the organization who recognize someone is in need of a physical, mental, or emotional boost.

Image 2.

*Reflective Pause:*

- *How does your workplace respond, with urgency, to an employee who exhibits symptoms of burnout?*
- *How does this organizational response contribute to your psychological safety as an employee?*
- *What actions do you need to see from your senior leaders to demonstrate an urgent response to symptoms of burnout displayed by an employee or team?*

*Notes:*

---

---

---

---

---

---

---

Sentinel responses are defined by several components. These components generally begin with an initial triggering event or recognition of need. Types of triggering events can include self-recognition of symptoms, concerns expressed by peers or colleagues, or leadership determination of a need for intervention. Once symptoms of burnout or compassion fatigue have been observed, an urgent and swift response should follow in a timely manner. The response to recognition of burnout should be reminiscent of the code blue medical emergency response for patients experiencing cardiac or respiratory arrest. Tangible and sustainable interventions to target the immediate need must be implemented. The interventions should be easy-to-access and use, and customized to the identified need. Longer-termed actions to address the post-acute needs of the individual or group should also be intertwined with an initial response. Evaluation of implementations should always follow intervention, to ensure appropriateness of resources and determine effectiveness of the resolution. As additional and easily implemented strategy can be use of a debrief method. Debriefs should be inclusive of time for reflective pauses to interpret learners' thoughts and feeling associated with educational content.

Additional forms of sentinel response can include interventions such as:

- A visit from the hospital Chaplain to offer spiritual services during a 10-minute break
- Create a relaxation room for staff to enjoy aromatherapy and use the five-minute massage chairs
- A brief walk on the track located on the perimeter of the hospital grounds
- Weight-lifting, batting cages, pickleball, or basketball courts on campus
- Emotional support from the organization's mental health counseling team
- Use of the education department's virtual reality headsets to play video games
- Dance therapy, art therapy, music (radio or having instruments to play), journaling, knitting, or other expressive movements

A significant contemporary contributor to healthcare worker burnout includes fatigue from inadequate staffing. This can be caused by a number of reasons, such as vacancies, employee changes in schedule due to call outs or not showing up for the assigned shift, or improper staffing tools. It is important to frame the narrative in the proper context as organizations are working to addressing burnout due to staffing concerns. Appropriate communication with teams regarding vacancies and turnover helps them to connect with the vision. Rather than debating appropriate staffing rations, nursing leaders and collaborative stakeholders must work together to critically appraise contemporary academic preparedness of new nurses. Additionally, it is necessary to work with boards of nursing to address the scope of practice limitations which are inhibiting teams from working more fluidly. Coaching individuals with chronic attendance issues can help erode staffing gaps due to callouts and no call, no shows. Use of peer-led hiring models can aid in reduction of attendance issues, since staff can set their own expectations with applicants, during the interview phase. Leaders are often overlooked when burnout pertains to staffing. However, leaders are quite vulnerable to burnout in the face of ongoing challenges with staffing their units as well.

When healthcare workers can tangibly witness the organization's commitment to timely and appropriate reaction to burnout, the trust environment is solidified. Caregivers should feel supported to activate protective wellness strategies without fear of their privacy being violated and their job being in jeopardy. Leaders should lean in to ensure their teams feel supported in seeking out assistance when needed. Appropriate response to burnout can determine whether an individual remains with an organization, or even impact their decision to stay with the nursing industry overall.

# Universal Efforts to Decode, Diagnose and Destroy Constructs Which Lead to Compassion Fatigue and Professional Exhaustion Syndromes.

In 2021, after being a practicing nurse for nearly two decades, I was inspired by the notion of proactive prevention. Proactive prevention involves the implementation of pathways to decode, diagnose, and destroy the many underlying daily threats to keeping an environment safe from burnout. Working with clinical nurses at the time, I heard daily about the devastating impacts of dealing with death and dying at an alarming rate. As a frontline clinician I also experienced the lived trauma of caring for patients who had a higher likelihood of negative outcomes or even death. In the face of insurmountable difficulties plaguing the healthcare industry, the idea of nursing resilience became both a key phrase and a trigger for unhealthy codependence on the nurse's ability to lean in and press on. Like so many times before, I – along with my coworkers – heaved myself into the work of providing clinically-sound, evidence-based practice in the midst of so much uncertainty about what was even considered to be evidence-based anymore (Figure 3). Proactive prevention disrupts the heave mentality and offers a different solution: avert. The elegant simplicity can be largely attributed to my prior knowledge gained during "my sabbatical" in which a primary function of my nursing role at the time was prevention of chronic health decline.

In the face of my peers and colleagues being heralded as heroes for our strength, I wondered why we were not instead fighting against the avoidable suffering to protect ourselves from burnout. Many organizations were not yet equipped to answer this question. Leaders were experiencing the same pressure to heave themselves into the work of keeping beds staffed with nurses to continue the care. In 2023 a new president was elected to the American Nurses Association. This new president voiced what so many of us had started to question as the healthcare hero label lay worn and dirty in the corner of nursing. It was clear there was a need for proactive prevention of burnout as we continued to recover from the lasting effects of a nursing shortage compounded by complex factors. Healthcare leaders and organizations must respond differently to challenges faced by nurses by implementing proactive strategies rather than waiting for burnout to ignite and reacting to its negative outcomes.

Recognizing, preventing and treating avoidable suffering of healthcare workers is an admirable cause to protecting the nursing industry. For decades, nursing has been regarded as one of the most trusted and ethical industries in the global workforce. Despite this, many nurses have lost faith in the organizations responsible for training, developing, and employing caregivers. Restoring this trust relies on bold and broad steps to protect healthcare workers from the heartbreak of becoming burned out in the field.

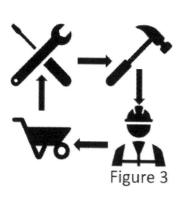

Figure 3

The systemic commitment to providing the support needed by nurses and caregivers is an essential ingredient to addressing the ever-present shortage within the workforce. Despite liberal efforts to bring awareness to the increasing demand for nursing care, greater effort is needed to tangibly and sustainably address the nursing supply chain. While burnout is not a new dilemma in nursing, the effects of recent strains on global healthcare systems has significantly underscored the damaging effects of this long-silent contributor to the caregiver shortage. Many reputable research models continue to suggest an increase in the gap between supply and demand for knowledgeable, skilled nursing clinicians.

*"There are times when it becomes necessary to break something in order to effectively restore it to its ability to function as designed"*

*– David Carter, 2024.*

Organizations must be willing to be transparent in diagnosing and categorically breaking the policies, processes and workflows which have continually nurtured the environment for burnout. The Center for Substance Abuse Treatment (US) published seminal work in the field of trauma-informed care in 2014 which comprehensively highlighted stress responses to harmful traumas. An important contributor in how a person responds to stress can depend on how the stressor is defined. The nursing environment of care is the theater of practice in which the worker performs duties associated with role functions. One contemporary factor which contributes to the environment for compassion fatigue involves nurses being subjected to repeated verbal, emotional, and sometimes physical abuse at the hands of patients or other consumers of nursing care. Often the nursing response to this type of stressor can include absorbing the abuse and heaving oneself into the work, only to experience more cyclical abuse.

Employers of nurses should identify potential risk factors for clinicians to be exposed to abuse, whether physical or otherwise. Identification of the risk must be accompanied by actions to mitigate the risk of harm to workers. For example, an organizational policy which concurrently restricts access to education and training in customer service or de-escalation, while expecting nurses to operate in tense and high-acuity clinical environments, can put employees at harm for abuse. Without being adequately trained in managing client or patient needs appropriately, nurses may inadvertently contribute to rising tensions, which later result in their own harm. Requiring employees to work in conditions in which they don't have available access to supplies necessary to perform clinical duties is another example of a systemic contributor to burnout. Failure to identify the lack of supplies as a contributor to workplace stress can lead to missed recognition of early signs of burnout, and also support an environment in which labor-intensive workarounds erode the resilience of staff by siphoning positive energy from the workplace.

An organization who fails to adapt systemic care models to the increasing health demands of populations served can also cultivate environments which are favorable to burnout. Leaders should routinely assess the workload of nurses and their unlicensed or interdisciplinary patient care partners. In assessing the workload, consistent awareness of staffing needs – either as a result of gaps created by vacancy or those created by the staff themselves – is paramount. A leader who recognizes a trend in a particular employee causing short-staffing because of repeated attendance problems is responsible and accountable to the team to address the poor performance in order to maintain balance (Figure 4). Identifying trends in staff being floated outside of their assigned duty station can give leaders the ability to diagnose more acute issues such as vacancies or changes in care demands. Finally, the leader must recognize how staff apply their own nursing knowledge into practice to ensure staff have the means to operate to their highest scope of practice. Nurses who are ill-equipped with supplies and appropriate staffing may find it difficult to operate as clinical expected.

More causative factors include poor protections against interprofessional conflict, failure to aptly support the needs of nurses to function at their highest ability, and uncontrolled imbalances in home and professional obligations. Nurses and care partners may disconnect

*What you permit*

*is what you promote*

Figure 4

with the work or the care environment as a protective measure when conflict is anticipated. For example, a nurse who is continually harassed by a provider who lacks the appropriate social skills to communicate effectively may choose little interaction with the provider as a protective measure. While this may seem harmless, this creates a break in communication that could potentially save a patient's life, thereby contributing inadvertently to the potential for missed care delivery and increased negative outcomes. In diagnosing the communication gaps of the provider and taking steps to mitigate the negative outcomes associated with these types of communication issues, the organization can then remove a systemic contributor to an environment which otherwise breeds burnout.

# Practical Application of Identified Solutions

Combatting healthcare worker and compassion fatigue will require efforts to close knowledge, skill and practice gaps relating to understanding burnout. Nursing can use information delivery methods and multimodal teaching strategies to develop high-quality and effective educational solutions aimed at shortening the divide from current to desired state. Examples of education initiatives to address knowledge or skill gaps include classes on the symptoms of burnout, podcasts which give a voice to nurses experiencing burnout, and introduction of strategies for caregiver resilience. Efforts to close skill gaps may consist of opportunities for nurses and leaders to demonstrate recognition of patterns in employee attendance, withdrawal of colleagues from the team culture of the workplace, or early physical symptoms manifested by coworkers – such as increased alcohol use or poor management of blood pressure. Opportunities for implementing practice strategies to define and recognize symptoms of healthcare worker exhaustion may depend on effective shared governance structures to offer a space for the employee voice to be heard in decision-making regarding institutional burnout policies.

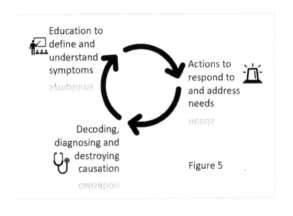

Education to define and understand symptoms

Actions to respond to and address needs

Decoding, diagnosing and destroying causation

Figure 5

Defining and recognizing burnout are the beginning of the cycle of removing this bizarre enemy from the workplace (Figure 5). Implementation of targeted interventions to address short-term and long-term symptoms of burnout is the next step in protecting nurses and nursing from the effects of compassion fatigue. Short-term symptoms of burnout can include irritability, tearfulness, emotional of physical tiredness, increased reliance on coffee or alcohol, and new onset of problems with physical health such as headaches or weakened immune system.

Longer-termed symptoms may include general disconnectedness at work, feeling dissatisfied or unfulfilled in one's role, poor and detached performance of duties, feelings of hopelessness or isolation, and clinically-relevant symptoms of depression or anxiety.

Quite possibly the most urgent of the approaches to eliminating burnout involves decoding, diagnosing and destroying elements of work life in which nurses must heave the load of physical and emotional exhaustion. Organizations have a duty to establish pathways to regularly review systemic contributors to burnout or potential for burnout. A practical application of this strategy can include conducting facility "wellness checks" routinely and in response to documented events. When evaluating the organization's financial status in relation to use of contract labor, integrate a mechanism for concurrent review of typical direct care and non-direct care workload. Study the amount of time it takes from an order for therapeutic treatment being placed to when it is completed and documented. This can give a greater indication of organizational health than simply to review the amount of spend on contract labor or reacting to missed productivity targets. Similarly, when determining the need for additional non-licensed caregiver support, research the contributors to acuity such as fall risks and patient combativeness to determine additional support levers which would alleviate or reduce strain.

Also, consider the amount of time caregivers are allocated for breaks and compare to the workload structure in place to support adequate decompression during time off. For example, what are the contributors to ensure employees have a restful and relaxing break to restore joy in their work day? Some facilities have taken measures such as removing any work-related educational materials from breakrooms and uninstalling alert systems from the breakroom so employees can have time away from alarms going off during their time away from the care environment. Executives can routinely review these types of elements to be more agile in addressing events or conditions which trigger a resilience response from their teams.

Involvement of key stakeholders using an honest diagnostic approach, and incorporating the caregiver voice in decision-making regarding prevention, recognition and treatment of worker burnout will pay dividends in reducing areas of the staffing shortage caused by nurses being unable to continue in the discipline. This can be accomplished by having a robust professional practice shared governance structure within the organization, and routinely sharing insights regarding burnout impacts and response outcomes with staff. Establishing and evaluating quality or strategic goals pertaining to burnout and employee wellness can also create a pathway for regular, recurrent review of organizational health.

# Strategic Analysis of Burnout Characteristics

Although it is atypical for the symptoms of burnout to be distinctively unique to an individual, how the symptoms manifest can vary between individuals or teams. Some influences which could lead to variation in presentation include demographics, such as age, generational identity, race, religion or gender identity. According to the American Nurses Association, approximately 69% of nurses under the age of 25 years old report feeling burned out, compared to nurses of older ages (2024). Other relevant factors can include practice area, clinical specialty, experience level, educational background, validated competence, environmental response, and even organizational reporting structure. Nurses who work longer shifts, pick up overtime, frequently work in areas exposing them to moral distress, and those who frequently change their shifts can be exposed to higher risk of burnout compared to those working in more stable environments.

These influences can sometimes be indicative or predictive of an individual's risk for and reaction to burnout. For instance, consider the demographic influences of a nurse of a given generation who has no prior clinical experience, as compared to a nurse of the same generation who has multiple years of clinical experience. Reflect on the risk of burnout for a nurse working in a level one trauma critical care unit, contrasted with a nurse working in a vaccination clinic. Leaders must ensure these implications are taken into consideration when establishing and applying a strategy to combat compassion fatigue in healthcare workers.

The strategy should include a methodical process of diagnosing burnout, while applying a layered or stratified system of response. In determining the severity and appropriate response to burnout, there are three concepts which could be used for classification (Figure 3). These areas of classification can include specific characteristics of burnout which can be useful in planning and intervening.

Firstly, the level of burnout may indicate a single, isolated person is experiencing burnout or could rise to the level of multiple individuals within a group who are suffering. In a mid-sized urban hospital, the chief nurse met with both a single individual with self-reported symptoms of compassion fatigue, as well as a team of licensed vocational nurses who verbalized feelings of inadequacy leading to burnout due to role confusion. At the individual level, a singular healthcare worker may feel isolated and disconnected from others, compared with a group of individuals or those with the same role. Homogeny in groups can be described as similarities in characteristics used to classify the individuals. Some examples include gender, role, age, race and experience level. This similarity can lead to compounded feelings of isolation as the individual workers empathize with one another's struggles, leading to an empathetic familiarity. The empathy experienced by one person or group of people can be intuited by those around them. This empathetic familiarity can also cause the individuals to have shared experiences, which can exacerbate the collective intensity of burnout. Role-based individual levels of burnout can present in job dissatisfaction, disengagement of the team, and of course attrition. If not carefully evaluated, leaders could mistakenly interpret a single role as not valuable to the organization's strategic plan due to misinterpreted outcomes of burnout.

*A county board of education implemented a care partner role within the healthcare structure of every school within the district. This new role was intended to augment the availability of clinically-trained staff to administer medications, complete simple treatments such as nebulization and wound care, and respond to behavioral emergencies. Because of ineffective* communication for how the role would be used in conjunction with the nurse and team lead roles, the individuals hired into the roles were often not used to their scope of practice. Feeling disconnected from the school board's mission and vision, care partners frequently took unscheduled paid days off and spent little time interacting with students. Each school reported uncertainty in the contributions of their care partners, and care partners tended to score less favorably on engagement surveys taken throughout the school year. After its first year, the care partner program was disbanded and the employees allocated to other departments.

The level of burnout in this scenario, while experienced by individuals within a given practice area, was seen in the same role of individuals across multiple sites. Instead of investigating the triggers to their disengagement and ineffectiveness, leadership made the decision to eliminate a program role which might have proven more valuable with identification of the causation of their symptoms.

Within a larger organization, each individual department or unit has their own identity and culture. When pertaining to burnout, the scope of symptoms contributing to healthcare worker fatigue can be isolated to a single area or be widespread across multiple areas. In fact, if left untreated, compassion fatigue can transfer across service lines and eventually shift organization-wide. Given the tendency of attendance problems and turnover as impacts of burnout, facilities often will share care delivery across departmental lines when one area is short-staffed or in need of extra support.

An example of this could be nurses being pulled from one team to another within a primary care clinic, or nurses being floated from one floor to another within a hospital setting. Leaders who fail to prevent or adequately address symptoms in one area can inadvertently contribute to staff from another area becoming burned out as well. Often this is seen in response to environmental factors such as poor staffing, high acuity, presence of bullying and other causative elements.

Intensity of burnout can range from a single episode or group of episodes of symptoms, to ongoing and widespread feelings of unhappiness and disengagement. An individual in a single service line can experience low-intensity, limited episodes of compassion fatigue when exposed to a given set of triggers. Under similar circumstances in a single service line, a team of individuals can display ongoing symptoms of healthcare worker fatigue and emotional exhaustion leading to burnout.

Figure 3

| Level | Scope | Intensity |
|---|---|---|
| • Can be isolated to a single person or role of individuals | • Can be isolated in a single department / service line, or widespread across multiple areas within the organization | • Symptoms of compassion fatigue may be limited and episodic, such as in response to certain triggers or events; or continuous. |
|    • *Example: LPNs, Paramedics or New Graduate RNs* |    • *Example: Nurses in various levels of leadership, teams working in critical care trauma, employees in adult and pediatric inpatient departments* |    • *Example: Teams show increasing symptoms of burnout when there is an increase in patients admitted to the unit for hospice care* |
| • An individual experiencing burnout may feel isolated, which can lead to rapid deterioration of symptoms and indicators of clinically-relevant signs of depression or anxiety | • Burnout in an isolated department can not only have negative effects on the culture of that particular unit, it can spread quickly to others when issues such as staffing lead to others cross-covering in the affected area | • Prolonged compassion fatigue could lead to turnover to another department, organization, or cause healthcare workers to leave the field altogether. |
| • A role of individuals experiencing burnout can lead to others being weary of the role itself, or to the elimination of the role due to perceived ineffectiveness | | |

**Methods to Overcome**: Ensure there are regular check-ins to assess for burnout, self-service resources which are easily accessible, rapid and effective stress-relief, and peer accountability to observe for signs and symptoms

In classifying symptoms of burnout, leaders and healthcare workers can use reflective questioning to stratify their actions. To determine the level of burnout, individuals can be assessed for symptoms of burnout in focus groups, during one-to-one interactions, on surveys or in other cumulative manners. If working with an individual, a leader may question "Who else is experiencing the same symptoms", "Who does this individual rely on as a support system", and "How is the person responding to what they are feeling". These questions may indicate the individual has negative adaptive behaviors which are either influencing, influenced by, or shared with their peers.

To evaluate the scope of burnout symptoms, an individual leader may collaborate with other leaders to review and compare data collected. This collaborative approach can provide the leader with support and also help the group of leaders to assess for trends. Questions which may be considered include: "What contributing factors could be putting the person or team at risk", "How frequently are others exposed to the symptoms displayed by the individual or team", and "What symptoms are evident across service lines or scopes of practice". Leaders should associate the level and scope of healthcare worker fatigue with an intensity score to ensure appropriate efficacy of their response.

# Future Implications and Important Considerations

Practical application begins with a thorough assessment of the organization's current status in efforts to prevent, mitigate, identify and alleviate symptoms of healthcare worker burnout. This can be accomplished using an array of tactics to explore the proactive measures of protections for workers, steps taken to close knowledge gaps regarding symptoms and impacts, and avenues for responding to symptoms recognized. As with any effective strategic plan, proper communication and messaging are also essential tactics. The future implications and considerations for addressing nurse wellbeing are far-reaching but also pose immediate threats.

**Important Considerations in Prevention**

To reduce the occurrence of burnout, employers can create educational programs to ensure awareness. Orient new team members on what defines the problem of compassion fatigue, using standardized language. It is important this language fits with the organization's mission, vision and values. The American Nurses Association provides a definition for burnout which can be used by those without a central vision on burnout. Professional development should be delivered in a multi-modal format to engage learners in a meaningful way, and highlight organizational outcomes in prevention and reduction of symptoms or impacts of burnout. As an example, in a system-wide attempt to address burnout, contact hours were applied in a one-hour class delivered to RN populations using the following problem statement, outcome, engagement strategies and evaluation methods:

## Prevention and Management of Healthcare-Associated Burnout

| Problem | Outcome |
|---|---|
| ᵣses continue to self-report ᵣnptoms of burnout at a rate of ᵣroximately 60% based on a ᵣ0 survey of RNs. Gaps in ᵣwledge of prevention ᵣthods continue to fail at ᵣeficial intervention. Nurses ᵣ self-identify symptoms of ᵣnout and use intervention ᵣthods to reduce or resolve ᵣings of burnout. | Expected outcomes:<br>1. 20% systemwide reduction in reported burnout symptoms within six months following completion of courses<br>2. 50% increase in use of level one burnout prevention tools, within six months of completion of courses |

| Engagement Strategies | Evaluation Methods |
|---|---|
| ᵣrners will engage in at least ᵣ:<br>  Case scenario review with group discussion<br>  Complete the Burnout Prevention Tools virtual scavenger hunt<br>  Pass the PMHAB escape room<br>  Write a reflective journal entry on burnout symptoms and use of the Burnout Prevention Tools checklist | Learners will participate in at least two:<br>• Case scenario review with completion of written discussion questions<br>• Complete the Burnout Prevention Tools virtual scavenger hunt<br>• Pass the PMHAB escape room<br>• Write a reflective journal entry on burnout symptoms and use of the Burnout Prevention Tools checklist |

Aside from awarding contact hours, nursing and executive leaders have other measures available to educate staff on this topic. Examples of alternative educational approaches include requiring all new hires to complete pre-work training sessions, conducting annual townhalls to educate on symptoms and resources while sharing data collected regarding organizational health, and inclusion of burnout topics in competency needs assessments.

## Important Considerations in Mitigation of Burnout Effects

Although preventive efforts are critically-important to protecting caregivers from the harmful effects of burnout, it is not fail-proof. When employees have been educated about symptoms and resources, it becomes essential to establish and maintain meaningful measures to reduce or resolve burnout that does arise. The responsibility to mitigate the effects of workplace burnout is multilayered and begins with the employee themselves.

*Employee Recognition and Response to Burnout*

Figure 4

Employees have the ability to be one of the first to identify signs and symptoms of burnout within themselves. Being educated about the symptoms and impacts of burnout sometimes are a later luxury in the life cycle of a healthcare worker's career. However, a mature organizational culture is inclusive of systems and programs to educate, acknowledge and react to burnout in a proactive manner. Healthcare workers experiencing compassionate burnout have often self-reported symptoms which may include exhaustion at a physical, emotional or spiritual level. Additionally, isolation and decreased satisfaction with the workplace culture of structure of the workload may be evidence of burnout.

The employee has a responsibility to check in with themselves frequently and to be cognizant of their own physical, mental or emotional barometer. This can be a brief mindfulness exercise in which the employee spends a few moments reflecting on current thoughts and feelings in relation to their work. Journaling and artistic expression are two ways of generating mindful reflection. These methods assist the nurse to confront their own feelings and potential symptoms. Self-awareness of one's own mental, physical and emotional response to varying workplace conditions and life stressors can aid the employee in developing or activating protective strategies (Figure 4).

Coping, or protective strategies may include:

- Activities which infuse positivity and energy, confidence and engagement of the psychosocial self-regulated response
- Physio-adaptive activities such as yoga, cardio exercise, strength training, meditation or stretching
- Methods to connect with others in a constructive and meaningful way, such as social events, family-bonding activities, teambuilding with coworkers, and joining a committee or shared governance council

*Peer Awareness and Escalation of Burnout in a Coworker*

Within the peer group there may be formal or informal assignment of roles which tend to complement one another. These roles may also counteract one another and can sometimes even create conflict on the team. An example might include the nurse who everyone looks to as the "caretaker" of the group, the care partner who is viewed as the "protector" of the team, the "collaborator" may be present, and even the "pot stirrer". Many variations of inherent roles may emerge within the group, as is typical of group cultures. While each employee may hold a special role or place as part of the larger team, every employee in a protective work culture has a responsibility to be on alert for how their peers are feeling and responding to workload changes.

Peers may use ways to check in with one another to both show they care about their peers while also as a way of connecting with others when they are experiencing self-identified feelings of burnout. Unit-based practice councils may be inclusive of methods to ensure touchpoints occur across peer groups. This could be illustrated by assigning "buddies" during work hours, establishing regular review of wellness resources available within the workplace, and scheduling group outings for connection with peers. Friendships formed may also help peers to connect at an individual or group level, creating an environment of trust in which employees may feel comfortable with experiencing feelings of burnout.

Coworkers can be on the lookout for signs of burnout in their peers, which may include: changes in mood or energy level, increased cynicism or tearfulness, changes in social behaviors such as alcohol use or eating habits, self-expressed feelings of burnout, increased verbal expression of unhappiness or disengagement with work, actively job searching, or other changes. These signs may be subtle or overt and can present differently in everyone. When witnessed, it is important for coworkers to consider their level of comfort in talking with their peer. If they feel uncomfortable or unsure about addressing burnout symptoms with a peer, the coworker has a duty to report their concerns to a frontline leader or trusted member of the management team. Despite this, it is equally important for peer groups to recognize they are never responsible or accountable for negative outcomes or impacts of individual employee burnout.

*Frontline Leader Identification and Action Against Burnout*

Leaders of healthcare workers should be required to have workplace-based training on the signs and symptoms of employee or team burnout, organizational strategies and resources to address compassion fatigue, and methods to identify or escalate their own feelings of burnout. This training ideally begins as soon as an employee assumes a leadership role, and should be repeated often enough to ensure ongoing organizational effectiveness at managing healthcare worker burnout. Frontline leaders tend to form close bonds with the employees and teams they lead. This can be advantageous when applying strategies to protect healthcare workers from the negative impacts of healthcare fatigue or burnout.

*Case scenario: Sydney was a charge nurse in a rural 75-bed hospital. Her daily duties included making staff assignments, helping her team to be compliant with mandatory education, assisting with orientation of new hires by ensuring preceptor assignments were consistent and compatible, and also managing burnout. Her unit manager had separated the employees into "teams", and each team was assigned a charge nurse as their immediate leader. Sydney had established regular check-ins with her team each month to ask about their wellbeing. Her standardized questions included: how they were managing their patients, any concerns they had about the types of patients they were caring for, and any questions they had about the distribution of assignments. She also asked her team about any changes in their home life, how they spent their time off, and how they felt they were fitting in with the team. When she received negative responses from her team, or indicators that there may be signs of burnout, Sydney uses a stratified reactive mechanism. She considers the level, scope, and intensity of the indicators (Figure 3). Based on these considerations, she demonstrates the process for activating the facility's wellness resources, shares her own experience with use of these resources, establishes a plan to follow up with her team or team member, and ensures timely escalation of her concerns to her unit manager.*

Sydney's scenario, while symbolic, is indicative of an effective strategy for frontline leader identification and action against burnout. She asks questions of her team to assess and diagnose any symptoms of compassion fatigue, or potential for burnout. She also has an organized and systematic plan for responding to observations of burnout. Sydney utilizes her information to intervene using the resources available at her level of leadership, and escalate quickly to her next-level leader. Finally, she evaluates the outcomes of her intervention by following up with her team. Her continuous and regular check-ins with her team ensure she keeps abreast of the team culture, can identify subtle shifts in the environment, and maintains an atmosphere of shared trust.

*Mid-Level Leader Responsibility to Employees and Teams*

Many roles exist within organizations to describe the role of mid-level leader. Some examples of mid-level leadership titles include nurse manager, unit manager, clinical coordinator or unit director. Generally, the mid-level leader has oversight of operations for an entire unit, department, or floor. Depending on the size or organizational structure, the mid-level leader may even have accountability for an entire service line or level of care, such as medical surgical, adolescent telemetry, bariatric critical care, pediatric medical, orthopedics, or others.

Mid-level leaders have accountability for the delivery of safe, high-quality, efficient care and services. This accountability is achievable by meeting the responsibility to maintain a safe, skilled, and competent workforce. The success of the mid-level leader can be dependent on the wellbeing of the individuals who comprise the workforce. Use of data, acute observation skills and authentic connection with their nursing teams can ensure leaders are able to react nimbly to changes in the department which indicate actual or potential burnout of staff.

*Executive Leader Accountability in Workplace Safety Culture*

Ultimate ownership for the workplace culture begins and ends in the administration suite, and with executive leaders. Measures to prevent, reduce and resolve symptoms and contributors to healthcare burnout make up the fabric of executive organizational oversight (Figure 2). Routine assessment of organizational status should be included in the executive strategic plan and bi-directional protective action should flow from the frontline to the highest levels of any organization. Tools and resources to determine organizational gaps can include overt measures such as surveys and connecting with staff. More abstract tools to assess the facility's needs may include reviewing data from clinical care outcomes, delivery of nursing services, and feedback from external stakeholders such as patients or clients. Executives should use indicators of organizational health status to influence decisions to respond to identified threats.

### ssessment of Organizational Status

- How are employees and leaders educated about what burnout is, how to detect it, and why it is important to mitigate?
- What gaps exist in how to respond individually and collectively when healthcare worker fatigue symptoms are identified?
- Is there a knowledge gap in how to respond to burnout of an individual vs an entire team?

### Determination of Organizational Gaps

- What triggers exist to indicate it is time to assess employees for evidence of burnout or compassion fatigue?
- How frequently is data collected to show utilization of protective measures to study resource impact?
- What tools are used to collect, analyze, and distribute the data?

### dicators of Healthy Organizational atus

- Employees feel safe to speak openly about symptoms of burnout and express security in leaders responding to their needs supportively.
- Leaders feel comfortable discussing the mental and emotional state of employees.
- Executives are consistently proactive in studying the health of the organization and responding appropriately.

### Responding to Identified Threats

- Stratified response mechanisms are based on the level, scope, and intensity of burnout symptoms identified
- **Level** of burnout can be an individual or team
- **Scope** can be isolated or widespread
- **Intensity** can be episodic or continuous
- Stratification will enable the organization to react appropriately

Figure 2

Executives have the power and influence to alleviate suffering at any point along the continuum of burnout. This is accomplished with the responsible use of organizational resources to address employee needs and maintain an atmosphere of trust. Awareness of gaps and effectiveness of existing strategies are responsibilities of the executive leadership team. Organizational officers should model and role model individual and team wellbeing strategies, while demonstrating their support for employees. Resources such as counseling services, grief support, teambuilding and engagement activities, professional practice councils, healthy use of employee time off, and ensuring employees have the tools and resources to work effectively are examples of executive support. Identification of bottlenecks to resolving needs such as equipment requests, IT support, environmental barriers, and staff shortages are all areas which should be routinely reviewed for gaps. Spending time to learn and understand the daily operational contributors to burnout can equip executive leaders to respond more robustly to needs. To sympathize with healthcare workers is not a strong response to avoidable suffering. Instead, focusing on sympathy and action can lead to better outcomes.

*Influence of Proactive Prevention Strategies at the Genesis of Healthcare*

While more contemporary research and scientific inquiry are necessary for complete discussion, there are additional areas of need for those who have not yet entered the workforce. Academic organizations have renewed their focus on adequately preparing students to be successful on licensure exams. Although a worthy concentration, schools of nursing and healthcare careers should integrate measures to prevent, identify and resolve compassion fatigue prior to future clinicians even beginning healthcare careers. This can be accomplished by integrating thematic support for student wellbeing and emotional support from the time students first express interest in license-based programs and training for unlicensed roles. Including these elements in training will not only prepare students for their future roles, but can have earlier effects in protecting their academic journey. Factors such as these can contribute overall to reducing the nursing shortage and protecting the future of nursing.

# Call to Action for Healthcare Organizations and Employers of Nursing Teams

Nursing as a discipline has foundationally shifted from its original foundation with the turn of the century. Generational motivations and societal influences have resulted in a redefining of the needs of the healthcare workforce. Multiple contributors to the nursing shortage have been amplified in recent years. Emerging as a more direct consequence of these contributors is the experience of burnout and compassion fatigue amongst nurses and interprofessional colleagues.

A collection of syndromes, the condition of worker burnout is characterized by early and late symptoms affecting the physical, emotional and mental wellbeing of individuals or groups. Typical signs or complaints include feelings of job dissatisfaction, disconnection from the team culture, physical or emotional exhaustion, deterioration in physical health, feelings of isolation or depersonalization, poor job performance and even clinically-relevant signs of anxiety or depression. These symptoms can be manifested in a number of ways including actual self-reports, outside observations, poor attendance at work, disjointed or cynical affect, job attrition or self-harm.

While many efforts have been made, there is still more work to be done to address burnout and its negative impacts to the nursing industry. Organizations must make intentional efforts to define the parameters of burnout to ensure teams are able to recognize the signs and symptoms. Education and training to reduce knowledge, skill or practice gaps are essential to the professional development of clinicians. These types of programs can equip nursing teams with the ability to protect themselves and each other from burnout. Sentinel responses to the clinical manifestation of signs and symptoms of burnout are needed to rebuild trust and reinforce organizational commitments to aiding healthcare workers in navigating the affects of burnout. The actions taken to address the needs of those exhibiting symptoms should be timely, coordinated, and appropriate to the specific situation of individuals and teams. Evidence from recent literature provides a roadmap of steps to take in synchronizing and implementing these types of action plans. Finally, a critical step in addressing healthcare burnout and work-related stress involves decoding, diagnosing and destroying the contributors to environments conducive to exhaustive compassion fatigue. Other the years, focus of organizational responses have been coordinated to help with nurse resilience and management of stress in the workplace. To align to the needs of the contemporary workforce, healthcare environments must be adjusted to identify and mitigate conditions requiring a resiliency response of nurses. This requires a concentration on continuously reviewing hard and soft worker conditions, analysis of direct-care and non-direct care tasks associated with nursing workload of direct care, and ongoing review of staffing conditions.

Initiatives to address burnout and work-related stress must be implemented to combat the ever-present nursing shortage. Nurses and employers of nurses have a responsibility to the public they serve to ensure stable environments of care. More research is needed in specific measures to identify and mitigate burnout conditions. Leaders and executives can use this practical guide as a reference point for establishing systems of care to protect and revitalize nursing pipelines.

While I have been a practicing nurse for many years, it was surprising to find that I could be at risk for losing the joy which had called me to healthcare. A multitude of factors came together to support my journey down this road. My experience was marked with physical and emotional exhaustion. Ethical concerns and moral distress were typical encounters in a normal work day. Due to attendance issues and variation in performance levels, my colleagues did not always create the most supportive environment. My leadership had identified me as "the strong nurse". Because of this, I was not always provided with the same level and frequency of one-to-one support as my peers. Ultimately, however, I owned my burnout. I can recognize with hindsight that I allowed myself to be overwhelmed by many external factors because I failed to be transparent in assessing myself for burnout until much later in my career. Even once I was educated on the definition and symptoms of burnout, without awareness of when to ask for help and what resources could help me, I continued to suffer in isolation. As caregivers, we often choose to pick up the load and continue to carry it along. At its worse, burnout even causes turnover and leads to many leaving the field in surrender.

It is important to frame the narrative of ratio-based care delivery in the proper context as we are working to address staffing concerns which may lead to burnout. Rather than debating varying definitions of safe staffing ratios, it is time we all came together to review academic preparedness standards, and work with our boards of nursing to address the scope of practice limitations which are inhibiting teams from working more fluidly. Nurses, we stand at the threshold of what will soon be healthcare history. Let's shake things up a bit..shall we?

# References

American Nurses Association (ANA). (2024). Nurse Burnout: What Is It & How to Prevent It | ANA (nursingworld.org). Retrieved from https://www.nursingworld.org/content-hub/resources/workplace/what-is-nurse-burnout-how-to-prevent-it/

Center for Substance Abuse Treatment (US). Trauma-Informed Care in Behavioral Health Services. Rockville (MD): Substance Abuse and Mental Health Services Administration (US); 2014. (Treatment Improvement Protocol (TIP) Series, No. 57.) Chapter 3, Understanding the Impact of Trauma. Available from: https://www.ncbi.nlm.nih.gov/books/NBK207191/

Chen, C., Strasser, J., Dent, R., Blanchard, J., Portela-Martinez, M., Muñoz, L., DeSmidt, B., and Perlo, J. (2024). How Can Health Care Organizations Address Burnout? A Description of the Dr. Lorna Breen Act Grantees. American Journal of Public Health 114, 148_151, https://doi.org/10.2105/AJPH.2023.307459

Christensen, A.J., Virnig, J.P., Case, N.L., Hayes, S.S., Heyne, R., Taylor, L.A., Allen, M.P. (2024). Addressing Burnout in the Primary Care Setting: The Impact of an Evidence-Based Mindfulness Toolkit, Military Medicine, Volume 189, Issue Supplement_1, January/February 2024, Pages 64–70, https://doi.org/10.1093/milmed/usad277

IOM (Institute of Medicine). 2011. The Future of Nursing: Leading Change, Advancing Health. Washington, DC: The National Academies Press.

Schmidt S.L., da Silva Cunha B., Tolentino J.C., Schmidt M.J., Schmidt G.J., Marinho A.D., van Duinkerken E., Gjorup A.L.T., Landeira-Fernandez J., Mello C.R., et al. (2024). Attention Deficits in Healthcare Workers with Non-Clinical Burnout: An Exploratory Investigation. International Journal of Environmental Research and Public Health. 2024; 21(2):239. https://doi.org/10.3390/ijerph21020239

Wang, L., Zhang, X., Zhang, M. et al. (2024). Risk and prediction of job burnout in responding nurses to public health emergencies. *BMC Nurs* **23**, 46 (2024). https://doi.org/10.1186/s12912-024-01714-5

# Appendix A: Discussion Questions for the Individual or Small Group

- **Discuss the last experience you had at work which brought you joy as a clinician. Reflect on the contributing factors which made this a joyful experience.**

  Consider the care environment, the types of patients you cared for, the personal connections you had with your peers and patients, what types of things were happening in your home life, and the support you felt from your leader to do your job.

- **Describe your understanding of burnout in terms of symptoms, risk factors, contributors, and potential impacts to your career as a clinician.**

  What are some of the risk factors which contribute to the development of burnout? What environmental, physical or emotional exposures can impact an individual's ability to cope with stress in a healthy way? If left untreated, what could be some potential implications of healthcare worker burnout and compassion fatigue?

- **Think about the characteristics which make you who you are. What are the ways these characteristics put you at risk for experiencing burnout?**

  These characteristics can include your age, generational identity, clinical experience level, specialty practice area, educational background, family and social factors, gender identity, and other factors.

- **Do a search of burnout symptoms and list them on a sheet of paper.**

  Circle the symptoms you have felt in the last two weeks of your work life. Rank them in order of severity, using a "1" for those symptoms you experienced daily for the last two weeks, "2" for those symptoms you experienced one to two times per week for the last two weeks, and "3" for those symptoms you only experienced once per week or less in the last two weeks. Place a line through any symptoms you have not experienced.

- **Talk to your leader or human resources representative about wellbeing support for employees. List the resources your organization has available to you as an employee, to protect you from burnout or assist you in overcoming burnout.**

  Place a check mark by the resources provided by your organization, which you have made use of in the previous six months. Place a question mark beside the resources you are not very familiar with or would like to know more about.

- **How do your coworkers respond to stressors in the work environment?**

  What shared risk factors exist between you and your coworkers? When was the last time someone on your team seemed isolated, disconnected, belligerent, irritable or unable to get control of their frustration with work? How did you react to this?

- **What are potential negative outcomes at the individual or unit level when individuals or teams experience burnout in nursing?**

  What can you do differently to protect yourself from experiencing the negative impacts of healthcare worker fatigue? How can you help your coworkers prevent, recognize or overcome symptoms of burnout?

# Appendix B: Discussion Questions for Leaders of Healthcare Workers

- What educational programs exist for employees, specifically relating to burnout, compassion fatigue, healthcare worker distress or employee wellness?

- What training is provided by your organization to prepare leaders to recognize, react to, and protect against symptoms of burnout in individuals and teams?

- On a scale of one to five, with one indicating not comfortable at all and five indicating expert ability to manage, how comfortable are you with recognizing, reacting to, and protecting against burnout in your employees?

- How frequently do you evaluate your employees for signs and symptoms of healthcare fatigue or workplace distress?

- What systems do you have in place for surveillance of burnout symptoms in your employees?

- When identified, what resources are available to help you address healthcare worker burnout as a leader?
- What gaps exist in equipping you to protect your employees from negative effects of burnout such as physical, emotional or mental exhaustion or illness?
- How effective are the resources available to you as a healthcare leader, in protecting your teams from burnout?
- What measures are taken to assess the effectiveness of resources used to assist you in responding to healthcare worker fatigue experienced by your team?
- What will you do differently, as a leader of nurses and nursing teams, to prevent burnout or respond to burnout in those on your team?

# Appendix C: Organizational Assessment of Burnout Symptoms in Healthcare Workers

| ıit /<br>ganization<br>ıme | Level / Type of Care Provided: | Team Makeup (Roles): |
|---|---|---|

| Organizational Assessment of Burnout Symptoms | | | |
|---|---|---|---|
| **Symptoms Present** | **Level** | **Scope** | **Intensity** |
| None Evident | ☐ None Reported<br>☐ None Observed | ☐ None Reported<br>☐ None Observed | ☐ None Reported<br>☐ None Observed |
| Minimally Recognizable | ☐ Individual<br>☐ Team | ☐ Individual<br>☐ Team | ☐ Individual<br>☐ Team |
| Moderately Recognizable | ☐ Individual<br>☐ Team | ☐ Individual<br>☐ Team | ☐ Individual<br>☐ Team |
| Extensively Recognizable | ☐ Individual<br>☐ Team | ☐ Individual<br>☐ Team | ☐ Individual<br>☐ Team |
| Contributing Factors (vacancies, turnover, engagement, tient needs, etc.) | | | |
| Resources Needed to ιddress Findings | | | |
| ιn for evaluation intervention and follow-up of employee / team response | | | |

Made in the USA
Columbia, SC
30 April 2024

35066590R00057